THE CHEAP SEATS

THE CHEAP SEATS

POEMS

BY

SCOTT POOLE

For Almeda,
You rule for a
Canada chic.
Good to know ya.

All the best
Scott
6/3/99

LOST HORSE PRESS
SPOKANE, WASHINGTON

Lost Horse Press

9327 South Cedar Rim Lane

Spokane, Washington 99224

First Edition

Library of Congress Catalogue in Publication Data

Poole, Scott.

The Cheap Seats: poetry / Scott Poole

p. cm.

ISBN 0-9668612-0-5 (paper)

I. The Cheap Seats   I. Title

PS3566.06237C48   1999

811' .54-dc21   98-53878

CIP

for Leslie and Ryan

He began to talk slow,
and his friends would listen to the delicious words
intently lengthing out
until finally
they would leave for the kitchen,
make pancakes,
and return to sit in front of him
as if he were the old wooden radio
they'd never had. He was happy
that they ate while he talked and his
words became sweet
and thick
till he could hardly lift them
from the long depth of his throat.
Finally, his lips began to crust over
with a heavy liquid,
and his friends were shocked
until they realized he had graciously become syrup,
and they poured it on their pancakes
and always thought of him fondly.

THE CROSSING

Crossing the Willamette, South bound,
eyes shooting forward,
I saw a cemetery
on a hill over the river
hiding in the trees.

I thought quick about how
I would sit on a headstone and throw
rocks down

to watch ripples slander out on the
moving curtain,

to stop with my wife, a lunch between us
and clouds wrapped with water and freeway
in a ribbon around us,

to know there were many with us
at this particular rest stop.

But as I crossed the river
the tombstones were not tombstones
but chimneys,
and houses all alike had grown beneath them.
It was not the death I had expected.

The drowsy feeling
of a bad day of fishing.
The ripples retreat into deeper curses,
empty water sails through the lines.

The old man still searches
the river's edge
picking up
anything
that will pay
for more time.

A fisherman
stretches back in his boat,
yawns and checks his watch.
His eyes glaze into a mirror of clouds.
A brain slips
from the back of his head
parting the river silently.

The ink of the water
percolates with bubbles.

Finally,
a tug
on the line.

ARMADILLO

She is wearing a silk blouse
and a tie, and earrings
and she is naked from the waist down
holding her underwear in front of her when suddenly, she
    sees a tag

that reads *Armadillo*.
Why did she not notice
this under the cellophane at the store,
before the clerk shoved her purchase into a bag and said
    "Is that all?"

And why did she not understand
the nervous man who rang up her lunch wrong three times
said sorry six, and how the hot beef soup
filmed over like her husband's face when he refused love

and stared at nothing, impenetrable
in a silence that nearly killed her. It gathers her into clarity
like whiteness, like underwear and long-nailed fingers, like
    freedom before
dressing. She knows what Armadillo means:
little armored one.

I have never been to New York
but I imagine all New York women
having long hair, long hair
they are always combing,
thick hair that gets loose
and crawls down the skyscrapers
in the static of the afternoon,
past the anxious,
the arguments,
flying with reflections of angels
sifting through rising souls
to finally fall over the faces of bums
napping between
hot dog carts
and heating grates,
drifting down through
dreams onto their
stringless violins.

PARADISE REGAINED

Are there any women left
who get naked in the forest?
I mean, is that kind of thing still done?

I've seen paintings.
They're old though. I mean,
I've never known anyone to disrobe in the woods

but myself. All of us
must do it:
walk right out between the trees, drop our pants and say, *well?*

A few leaves rustle. Somewhere
birds chirp. An insect buzzes
quietly beside a nipple.

Some part of me will be sorely sad
if I never come upon a naked forest woman,
if I never have the chance to witness

breasts thrust toward the mountains,
pink buttocks fooling around with sunlight,
palms upright as if asking, *what now?*

That's when I want to walk up and shake hands,
congratulate her, take off my fig leaf pants
and say *we finally made it back. Didn't we?*

THE FISH VIEWING ROOM AT BONNEVILLE DAM

One of the most romantic places in the west.
One of our first dates.
Children dance quietly on blue carpet.
The only light is the stained-glass
of the river.
In whispers
the eels
pray with little sets of teeth.
The last salmon in the world
glide over your head
slow as a kiss.
And the Columbia
is reduced to
the thing said
when you can think
of nothing else.

CRIPPLED WOMAN IN A FIELD, OKLAHOMA 1933

I remember the thinness of her ankles
and the wisp of dress,
elbows strained at bad angles.
Would the house burn before her eyes?

A small crackle might start about the porch
and a ghostly face of smoke send her
to contend with sky.

She feared the braces on her legs
would harvest lightning.
I remember one tree creaked
and the lawn stretched with shadows
toward thunder.

In her one hand she held a strand of wheat,
fibers, hairs,
infinite marks and turns . . .

Looking up she saw a field of
millions like the one in her palm.
I remember her reaching out
to the solid air.

The crickets seem
to be breaking legs tonight.
And pieces of violins
float under the bridge downtown.
A brick falls from the library
and no bird flies in.

On the back wall of the burned
out school, the painter brushes
a red cloud into the sink
of an imagined smile.
From the edge of a field
a child runs off into woods.

And as you hear a knock on the steel
furniture, steps on the hardwood
stairs, a brushing against the bare walls,
what burden will assail you, in the throat
of this unexpected noise?

WHY ARE YOU FAT?

I always wanted to live
in the land of fat grapes, fat cows
and fat thick bridges,
bridges so wide
they built houses on them.
Houses where people woke
to the violence of the stone ribbed river
and ignored it. A happy place
where people packed
in swollen stucco rooms
to eat
sausage fried in lard
potatoes slopped with butter
and deep-fried Mars bars.
It would be a land where people lived
drank thick wine
and sang out their guts
until they rolled into rivers
and were gone, without embarrassment,
without collapsing in a
thin street blocked by strangers.

A minute ago, I kicked
my leg through the wall.
I quit, see. No cares.
Maybe the relief of rain.
Is that the breath
of a great dane
or is it the wind off a frog pond?
Insects
under the skin? In here
cramped with loose paper,
food crumbs, clothes in drifts
along the hall, my body heat
has broken its light bulbs.
Out there it's the same as flying,
or the reason why dogs plunge
heads from car windows
when there is nothing to see
but tears.

THE MIME'S LAST DAY

An old couple follows him now;
they wait in the park, and then they start.
"That's no box," the old man says,
"that's a wet bag.
Why don't you put your head in it?"

The old woman with her manicured drawl
thinks the mime needs reassurance;
"It's not that we think you pull a bad
invisible rope, it's just that
you're pulling something, well . . . let's say
kind of perverted . . . if you're going to pull it
like that, I mean, what will people . . ."

But the mime has prepared
the black hole rocket maneuver
an original in the silent histories of mime.
He crushes himself to launch position:
a black disk on the pavement.
The couple doesn't know what to say.
He really does look like an empty hole.
Investigating, the old man steps too close and plunges in.
The old woman grabs for his arm and is sucked in after.
A yelp spreads pigeons across the world;
the mime leaps up screaming and never really stops.

THE TROPHY

The quarterback jogs backward into a patch of light
looking so young with his team in the lead.
He's got all the time in the world and throws the ball
in a perfect arc beyond the screen.
I follow it left of the television, to the little lamp
rescued from Grandma's garage. Its genie bottle
base glows happy in cherry wood under the dark
orange shade. In a picture, from the first days
of our marriage, we hold this lamp
between us, in front of our first apartment
which resembles an abandoned equipment shack:
rust slides from the slats of the house,
the front door is unpainted metal. We are smiling.
It's a perfect fall day right after the August wedding.
There's a spirit like the men on the screen, who cheer
and jump around with their helmets and endless
protective gear. We seem naked in comparison.
We thought we'd escaped our youth untouched,
the lamp between us like a stupid trophy.
The other team takes the field, and they look older
and tired. You can tell they've quit already, and shadows
of their fumbled hope fill the stadium.

Again it's either fishing or a bad movie.
You've lost your car keys. So fishing it is.
You walk the dust near pines
doing your best to appear.

In town you see that someone has mistakenly
replaced your office with a coal mine.
Successful company men sluice from the gates.
You spoiled your childhood. You thought it great,
under beds and in closets.

At the stream you fall asleep, certain there must be
a beautiful woman in a tree somewhere.
The fishing line falls drunk into the water.
At noon, your sandwich runs away.
Again, you realize this is no documentary.

You try suicide, but swallow the gun
and end up vomiting hot sand.
You finally catch a trout, but it's ugly and insecure
and you can't bring yourself to eat it or throw it back.
In the suicide note you misspelled
"me." Coal dust covers the sun.

The river goes home. Anyway, you think
how wonderful. Or at least . . . nothing.
The trout agrees and looks up
at your jaw in amazement.

CHARTRES

This is how the fantasy goes.
I have this thing
about standing in front of Chartres at sunset,
with coat and camera.
I'm saying wow like a mantra as the
stone and glass arc infinity,
but as always
I begin to hear yelling in French
from the near neighborhood,
echoing through the perfect buttresses
over money or eggs or eggs and money—
who bought the eggs or who didn't
buy the eggs or who never buys the eggs.
In French it sounds beautiful
and as always
it's a noise in the world I don't expect.
I fall in love. My skull is cast
blue with old symbols.

THE SECOND COMING

The other day I found the moon in the couch.
God must have dropped it when he came over.
He hadn't shaved. It seems luck had run out
and he felt things were starting to slip.

As I picked the moon up, it was cold
and beautiful and I was entranced
but then it began to melt. I panicked,
put it in the freezer
where it stuck to the shelves,
I couldn't pry it out.

Now, I'm having all kinds of trouble with the freezer,
it starts to overheat
and whine and make horrible ocean noises
every 28 days or so.
I can't get any sleep.

To top it off
I don't think the moon likes me anymore.
And I suspect
it's still illuminating in secret.
I spend most nights opening and shutting,
opening and shutting
the freezer door.
God. I hope He doesn't show up
again.

BACK OF AN OLD CHINESE MAN
IN BASKIN ROBBINS

There are a million
emperors in his gray
black bristles.
A million temple columns
in his tendons
descending
into a white collar.
A million little hopes
mill around in his hands
that smile and turn into robes.
Fireworks of spring parades
have turned his fingertips
to ash.
His tired slacks
reveal small old ankles
leading a million feet.
A million have come to this tile floor
to this summer
to this orange sherbet stain.

HONEYMOON

The feeling of a cocktail party in heaven
passing drinks in and out of a vortex,
as loaded cruise ships pull in after

Hurricane Juanita has destroyed the hot dog stand.
Wieners litter the deserted beach
like the lopped fingers of gods.

The terrorists slow to graceful.
A girl points out benefits of destruction
while pulling buns from a fallen tree.

A boy lies back near her
where dark streams roll out from the mountains.
He says casual things, filling his mouth with mud.

"Sometimes life is a horrible
hard salami sandwich on a white plate.
I'd travel miles to see a parrot blown apart."

They swab the empty skin of beach-side mansions.
Everyone who goes in says "hell-o," squinting
to see, as if they know where they are.

THE SPOKANE ANGELS

In front of the hotel, a knot of old men
lie against the cold brick laughing
and I wonder why angels are young and fat
in oil paintings. If we could truly see angels
above this city of snow, perhaps

they would be these old men
naked, swimming around each other ·
in barren sunrises, their horribly strong bodies
cutting the air with hollow-boned wings.

I would wish for them naked old women
who pluck apples from shopping bags.
Because they were the angels
they would eat fruit, bring lovers together,
and help the cub scouts.

Only the truly ethereal could be beautiful in this frost.
I am happy at sunset to see them
again at rest in their clothes
keeping a tight vigil
between street and hotel
immaculate in the tides of rush hour.

Watching a kayak crawl the zigzag of explosions
on this July 4th, I can't help think of you still
at the bottom of the lake. We've been assured
you won't float up during the boat parade,
but as your eyes evaporate, children stay off the water.
They say you were an A student. Did you think of Ophelia,
the power she had to turn Denmark mad in act four?
In a dark boat house, a man with a water-stained hat
mumbles, "Someone has to dive down and get her."

Through clean trees and hills shuddering off heat
and the failed gestures of bottle rockets over an empty skiff,
I see you dropping dimensional in trout, sunfish and vines
your dark nipples and purple folds issuing
a wet command, beating the vein valves,
writing the rules in this good night of bass notes
and lake bottom mud. I know you caused the rain.
We run out of fireworks early. Your last order escapes.
A bubble breaks the surface between the deep black
and the languid attention of smoke-filled pines.

COLD CALLS

This is not my area.
The street is a hallway of silence. The yard's
gone. Small houses surround
weak, pressing against the squares of orange
lamp-light. No animals.
A porch leans to the left.
Faintly, a phone next door
moans through the wall unanswered.
There is that sound of wind in leafless trees,
always. My shoulders
ache, they steam in the feeble light
of stars assigned here
as punishment. The porch light is off
like a lie. It speaks an absolute
nothing. I'm ready to go home now, but I stop.
Dangling in the heavy rectangle of the door
is a set of keys.
There must be at least fifty of them.
I listen for anything.

A lamp burns in the hot breeze.
Eight people walk in on a tour
carrying paper. They stop at my desk.
I notice the sweat stain on the leader's shirt.
He moves his arm around
describing my features.
I could be having a heart attack,
so slow
I might never die.

Someone throws an octopus on my face.
I feel the cold disk of a stethoscope
where nothing grows.
"It's still moving," the man says.
The group begins singing,
Haydn. I can sense
the octopus likes it.
Then someone is going down on me.
I let them,
I don't want to fail.
I'm not sure whether I'm dealing
with a man or a woman.

But soon my inspector withdraws.
The octopus is removed
and the tour moves on
to the next desk.
"How did you do?" my coworkers ask.
"I couldn't tell you."

That summer night, outside the building
five thousand people are playing sports.
An executive in a baseball coach's uniform
is rummaging through bushes.
"What are you looking for?" I say.
"Oh, there you are," he says,
and pulls my heart right out of my chest.

"Thanks," he says, and waves the heart
at children in the distant field.
He throws it hard into the blue.
I squint, but as usual
I can't see where it's going.

Twelve miles to go and the cow doesn't care.
It's raining. In her eyes the same disbelief
as in passing drivers' faces. I keep up this running
because of the patient's split chest,
how hard the heart bucked in its banana cream pudding.
This is an unhealthy heart, said the voice of the health film.
The cow can't imagine its own inside. Maybe that's why
cows won't run. Last year's fields soaked
through and the cows began to sink. Tractors strained,
laying timbers, breaking legs with chains, while
heifers in the back fields quietly disappeared.
When spring plows came, blood ran from the ground.
I imagine the mud-hungry earth, crushing
a cow's ribs, its breath, as I climb this hill.
How far have I gone? I think of the cow
alone in quicksand, swallowed
by a lost sureness, not knowing how to be lighter,
waiting for vibrations to shake the ground,
for something above the body to descend,
for escape.

ROLLS OF QUARTERS

Through the shadows of leaves
dying on a tree
in street light I walk
thinking of laundry
and another week

waving from
the back of a convertible
heading west,

and me with arm raised
a basket on my hip,
feet melting into pavement.

I know many things are left
undone.

But on this spring night
desperate violists
dance hard
by the railroad
tracks.

And if there is music,
hope might be down there
too.

A strange joy can be heard for miles.

We watched the salmon we caught drunk
soak like sacks of eyes in the deck's rain,
I had to turn off the light, so I could hear.

I could only wait it out with my friends now—
the acid breathing of our throats,
the refrigerator's brown decisions,
and the darkening stained glass
filling like an organ with fog.

The next day the fish were gone.
I thought it was a gift I had survived
when I saw Schmidt tilted like an old pier
weaving on the water-skimmed beach
in low-tide rain with scotch and coffee
looking for fish, swearing intricately,
shadowed by twelve white ducks
and all their beautiful feet.

The other day I saw a large houseplant
in the back seat of a Cadillac as I
was on my way to the unemployment office.
I remembered the times I envied
those who were chauffeured.
Perhaps the plant was being driven
to a nice professional office
to keep the nonprofessionals calm.
Suddenly, I wanted to be that
plant, to be chauffeured,
to remain true to the organic call.
I could be helpful
by sitting with those in trouble
fanning them, placing a frond on their shoulder.
I wanted to say,
"I won't lie.
I know I can't help you, and it won't
cost you anything, either.
Take a look at me, inhale
my green breath,
take a look!
Sometimes
things work out."

My foot on the gas pedal
grows deeper
into the car,
the road, and time
passing beneath my fallen
arches. Toes
limp but
aware as bees
waiting out a storm
with no more
energy than it takes to
rest on a pin
head. My foot drips
honey. This little Piggy
checked into a Zen center
and never came home.
My foot,
taking me away
in a blooming of
machine, man,
and my minor parts.

I guess my Grandfather was supposed to be dead,
except the last time I was at his house
he was still there, not in a coffin, but a chair
surrounded by thousands of potted flowers.

"All these flowers, it's a damn shame
people don't have better things to spend money on."
From under the chair he produced a hammer,
"Start smashing, kid!"

We destroyed that room,
we ripped and tore till each arrangement
was spread out naked on the rug.
Grandpa brought in the hose
and washed every petal down.
"You could spray and soak
and not one of these colors would
bleed unless you touched it."

So we filled our arms with bouquets,
rushed out to the wood chipper
and shot clouds of petals
raining roses, hyacinths and carnations
over several sullen blocks.

The old neighbor with blue and pink in her hair
came to scream through the fence.
"You were supposed to be dead. A lot of people
are going to be mad you're not dead!"

"Shut up you old bag! I'm dead enough!"
and he shot a storm of nasturtiums at her.
The sky turned a twirling red.
Over the whir of the machine, torn
chrysanthemums bled laughter.

I was sitting under a tree.
You called me a loser
and told me to leave.
Feeling dumb, I did.
You cut down the tree
to help make a log cabin.
I came over commenting
on the country atmosphere.
We talked
and had pine needle tea.
Being comfortable
we quickly got bored
and decided to organize
an environmental march.
We made signs out of
your paper
and cut sticks from
your woodpile
and marched
but no one noticed
and the effort quickly died
so we got drunk
and watched the march
on tv.
Then you fell asleep,
dropped your smoke
and your house burned
down.

CEMENT PEOPLE

The cement people arrive, fall onto the flowers
and break them, breaking themselves.
Every morning we find them
in the beds, staring dumbly upward.

You can't stop them. They try to touch the flowers,
beauty seeps in and they crack in half.
It's hard for me and the boys. We spend all day
rolling bodies out of the garden.

The cement people, what are they thinking?
Aren't their beautiful rooms enough?
Why not grace a gallery or a country club
quietly, without this tragedy?

Why this nightly basal mania? Will we
never have a shortage of gray limbs and frozen lovers
for the highway department crusher? The flowers
keep growing, unaware of their power to torment.

For hours my mother had been
digging the wrong furrow.
It had looked like the right furrow
when she started
but somehow
it became a circular furrow. So
she started another furrow
inside the other
and soon the new furrow had turned
circular too
just smaller. She looked around,
then began another furrow
and that one became
just a circular blob
in the middle of the other two furrows.

"Shit,"
she said,
and sat down
right in the middle
of her bull's-eye.
She produced a harmonica
and began to play the furrow blues.

I went up on the roof of the barn and sure enough
if any bomb was looking for a target
it would have no trouble finding
this furrow in which
to plant itself.

But, the way she blew that harp
made the furrows feel good
like they were rippling out from her,
rather than circling in. I could see
the whole land knew what she was playing,
the whole land had been planted all along
in the waves of this target blues.

I thought, how could this be
the wrong furrow?
I came from this furrow.

Desert caravans are leaving
down Gerdaldo street.
The moon fights
the palms for sky.
And I,
on my red
verandah,
listen to Miles Davis fall
out of the desert pines.
Empty cocktails line
the railing. A generalissimo
pigeon struts among
them trying to impress.
A commanding voice calls
Ready, Aim, . . .
I kick those glass soldiers off the railing
and they fall, wounded.
The pigeon flies off, shitting
delicately
on the neighbor's roof.
A paper boy recedes
down the hill, he turns pink
and waves as if
it's right after the war.

You know getting a job is not good enough
that having a house with a working car is not good enough
when the mortgage is due, and you pay it, you're not making it,
and even if you make it, accolades pour in,
and people name their children after you—it's not good enough.
The working car will break, the job suck you inside-out
the rent keeps increasing, and a few minutes are chipped here
and there, those accolades will end and those children
will go to jail and blame you for selling out
so my advice is to
start little fires out of just about anything.

Burn a match, then a toy soldier, then some moving vehicles.
Burn down an outbuilding, then
a topiary. Carry a magnifying glass to distinguish the details.
And when you light fires notice details
burn to a common ash called hope.
This is what hope is in the bottom of the heart my friends:
burnt details.
Don't let hope
rise to your heart.
Keep it in the guts where it can chew, pinpoint
and start the little fires.

WATCHING FROM BEHIND THE
WATERFALL OF MY PORCH

Small lungs of leaves. Dark soaked hedges.
Across the street, a girl
in the square fog of her lit porch.
Cars flow between our houses. The rain ripples
the plastic siding through which
a mother calls to a father in
the amazing steam off her wet sweater.
She is drinking her dad's beer alone,
and suddenly laughs. The sound is honest.
How I admire
the rain in her private room.

It's midday
and because a woman said
you're buried in happiness so you never think of mine
he stomps down the street to her house
to give her his happiness lamp.

The cord drags along the asphalt
and for some reason he knows
when the orange terrier emerges from a vacant lot
it's coming for the plug,

so when the terrier bites down and
the lamp turns on,

the man has to laugh,
the dog to bark,
because there is no other way to see this joy
under the jealous weight of the sun.

I KNOW WHY THE APPLAUSE PLANT GROWS

The other day I was riding a show pony
around in my mobile home. The bravest
pony that ever cantered in a trailer.
And I let it rumba where
it wanted, capriole in the kitchen,
and triple-axle the bathroom wall.
Then the National Guard came home
and said, "Get that goddamn horse out of this trailer."
"But this is intermission," I pleaded.
And they got hot-iron mad and threatened
to throw steak knives in the second act.
But I didn't care. You should have seen the way
that horse leapt lovingly up and down my hall,
as the applause plant grew higher and higher.

SATISFACTION

I never thought this would do it, but
now, screwing the handles
back on the soup pot,
I feel almost satisfied.

I've never been almost satisfied before.
So I look out the window
at the leaning bending Ponderosa. How wonderful!
I don't want them straightened.

They pose for me as the new colonnade
to a future cathedral
not a sterility of flat stone but
a sanctuary of smoke
and smells like those of the first cave
with its first soup.

Yes. Now, while I
screw the handles
back on the stupid soup pot,
the handles I didn't even know could
fall off,
I am almost completely
what I never supposed
I might be.

I walk out to go to work
and a guy is sleeping in my car.
So I open the car door, get in
and slam it shut.
"Hey, where's my money?" The guy blurts
banging my head on the steering wheel.
"I don't have your money!
Get the fuck out of my car,
I have to go to work!" I say.
"Work?" He asks.
"Work," I say.
"Then you can pay me the money
you owe me tonight," he says.
In the bent rear view
I look at him, he looks at me.
So I kick the door open
and go inside.
I wasn't going to argue with myself,
that's my secret.
I call work
tell them car trouble
yes — all day.
Then I go back to bed smiling,
for the first time that week
to the soft sound of him ramming
the car into the garage.

We were making young love
in the balcony when the two old men
wandered in to move the mountains.

"Why do they always wear red gloves
in the summer?" She said.
"I don't know," I said,
and I didn't know, too.

The two old men pushed the first mountain
up from the second mountain
then stored the second mountain
behind the great folding chairs of the north.

"I love their sun hats," she said.
"Oh yes, they *are* wonderful," I said.

After they punched in a few trees,
they pushed the sun down,
and with the sound of pulleys
the room faded and became cheaper.

"Now, that's just beautiful," she said.
"It is something," I said.

The old men left and the lights
of a young city popped on, then off
like a fallen Christmas tree.

"Wait, where are they going?"

"Why *do* they wear red gloves in the summer?"

In the future there will be eighty-year-old
porn stars.
I could retire with them.
Watching their bodies under
simple old lady dresses.
Wandering the building with a slow gait,
one hand stroking the wall,
mouth open,
drool falling out.
And seeing their eyes turn on subjects
of love and photographs.
It would be wonderful
with a mug of coffee,
giant old house by the woods.

I would want each to have an advanced degree
and to sit on old couches,
talking of Schopenhauer, Holmes
Thoreau, and Fudd.

Maybe there would be no talking,
just the sounds of birds
on the screen porch
three days deep in July.

Maybe just a slow gathering
of images:
hands cooking,
mustached lips, smiles,

feet in nurses shuffling shoes.

We would all enjoy
the quiet way a leaf might talk, a fig leaf perhaps,
the symphony of a forest,
among bodies that have survived
almost Olympic training,

the old porn stars and me.

BREAKING DOWN

If you wanted
to get in my truck
you had to pound the door
just below the handle.
Taking corners, the dash
lights would flicker
like a broken marquee.
Its red color was pale
in many places where
various chemicals had
poured from the bed.
The turn signals
were crossed, so
I was taught to think
backwards. Stepping
on the gas,
you had to anticipate
a three-second delay.
Stepping on the brakes,
you just had to anticipate.
The temperature gauge
always hovered near outrage
so it was a challenge
planning a route
to remain cool.
And when orange
rusty water began
seeping from the engine,

I sold that truck for fifty
dollars. But, while cleaning
it out for the first time ever
I found the rolling noise
that had charmed
me for four years:
a can of beer under
the passenger's seat.
The can was silver,
all the color rubbed
clean off from hundreds
of trips across the state
to see you, but still
it was unopened.
And although the beer
was horrible and warm
(you knew I had to
drink it), it was
like the first time
you let me kiss your neck—
when I told you
we had broken down
and you pretended
to believe me.

I was just walking through your park, and had a few questions.
Why take the leaves off and put them up every year?
How come there are no good animals around
when there are squirrels you didn't need in Hawaii,
and a stray cat too lame to prowl India?
Near the slough is a dog that sounds almost like a bison,
that's cool. You still send Cougars to invade the city! Thank you!
And what about the way a ripple will rise
for no reason, on a pond. Is there a bonus for noticing this?
Maybe I will kneel here and lick the leaves, or maybe
just hold them close. Do you mind?

TO MY FIRST LOVE

As my scrotum falls away from my leg
I think of you and your blonde hair
and how you couldn't drive
and that poor old woman you nearly hit on the way to
    the country
and your beautifully inept way of
holding my erection and looking out the window
like a friend with one hand on a doorknob
stopping to say one last thing
before good-bye.

TACITURN

She is taciturn—
that means not wanting to talk.

Socks under the bed.
The back of her head.
The mailman delivering a bill.

If the snow you thought was beautiful
ate at your shoulders
it was probably salt,
you were probably a slug.

Later, I carried the garbage
into a cold street full of cats.
I stood there until
frost slept on my tongue.

This silence is nothing but me.
It drowns things too small to hear.
It's a little car running out of gas
nowhere.

THE OCCASION

When I die,
there will be a napkin in a glass
somewhere
behind some relatives
beat and tired
looking at their watches
eating,
drinking . . .

My pine box will be in the corner;
I will be admiring the ceiling,
as I did in third grade while standing
in the corner, looking up . . .
And perhaps even on it
will be the napkin in a glass,
beer in the bottom
gathering in the napkin
escaping and spreading out
as a circle soaks into the coffin.

Perhaps someone will be
laughing by the door.
A belly of a man will be there
smoking cigarettes
watching the traffic of
black cars stuck
in a July heat.

Some child, alone in bed
dragged out through that smoke
will later wonder
if I was hungry.

Every day from my porch I search
the amber forest of insect wings.
Something's in the fence, rusting
nails that hold privacy
together. It comes up like a child—wide eyes
at the bottom stairs. It's an edge
of the house's smile. *What are you?* I say,
come in already! But it just peeks
from my cuticles.
I say quietly
sometimes breath opens
a door that isn't there. Clinched,
I wait like a lemon.
Can you help me?
The power lines have fallen
over the field. Every once in a while
blue sparks
illuminate the wandering physicians.

A PAIR OF SOCKS

The sun casts a spotlight on the wall
though we're not famous.
Still I walk out and shovel the deck of snow
and say to no one, "Come in and see the dancing."
She reads the paper,
makes eggs.
I enter with coffee.
Invisible tourists file in behind me.
I fry some sausage and become sausage.
I slice bananas and become bananas.
She pours a ridiculous
bassoon of orange juice
and jigs elegantly.
A few pictures are taken.
I sit at the table
and become the table.
There is no applause
and the tourists depart.
I hear her cleaning the back bedroom.
The washer and dryer depart.
It looks like we'll pull ourselves from nothing again
like a pair of socks from a drawer
made far away by famous men.

CHARLES MANSON'S MOM

We've all had a brush with fame
and while talking to my wife's grandmother
she casually mentions that Charles Manson's mom
used to live across Montgomery street,

not Charles, he was in prison in Seattle,
and Charlie's Mom (a real nice lady) sent him a guitar
that he smashed to shiny shards
because it wasn't the brand he preferred.

Of course then there must be a guy,
drinking a beer, telling his relatives
yeah, once I picked up the pieces
of the guitar Manson broke

and I didn't think much of them
because he wasn't famous yet,
didn't have the swastika and so forth
so I put it all in the trash. And so

a cousin tells his friend
that his uncle once picked up
pieces of the guitar that Charles Manson broke
over the head of a guard while trying to escape jail

and somebody's friend sits down
with his guitar (which he didn't break) and composes
a sonorous three chord blues riff in the style of Johnny Cash
about the broken guitar escape attempt of Charles Manson

and like the bulldozer that roared
through landfill garbage
to dump Charles Manson's guitar, Charles has cut
a clear path through our lives.

Thanks Charles. Thanks for being
famous.

The paintings in my house are distances to be crossed.
Wyeth's cripple stares across the field at
Van Gogh's night café. You can hear voices.
Hopper's people concerned with unnamed destinations.

Looking around I see a table, the rug,
yellow ceilings, and a sponge by the battered sink.
This is my own picture waiting for me,
but I refuse to pose.

So the sponge grows until it's leopard-sized,
and it pads over and stands on my chest.
I laugh at the pink monstrosity,
but I see that it's soaking me in.

And it's not about to attack,
it *has* attacked, and its eyes
are like the spaces between buildings.

I walk down a wet hallway,
turn left and right, try not to notice a door.
The water rises and there's no way back.

It took ten hours in a twenty-year-old truck
to reach the coast. And when we made it
Jesus drove right out to the dark hard sand.
Deliciously, I fell out flat onto
my back and took a pull of wine.
For hours we watched the stars
and I believed I was flying them all
like kites. At dawn, when the
sun was wading in the sea
Jesus said, "We can be gods whenever we want."
A woman on a dark horse was taking
her morning ride. I don't know if she
heard the statement but Jesus
ripped off his tunic,
ran after her, threw her off the horse, hopped on
and galloped down the beach
mixing screams with flying hoofs
and ocean roar.
Later, the police
cars chasing him formed a halo of light.

There's a small man who walks echoed alleys
out on the perimeter
below our windows, tethered in heat,
twirling a yellow bullet-ridden umbrella.
There's furious light below the brick
flowing in his old clothes and
he's alive as a brave flamingo, alive as
a cigar.
I don't know,
the faces of people are wet useless streets,
but his umbrella
and the bright things in my apartment wink at me,
though the lights have been desperate for hours.

THE DIET

Friday night, the moon
sits on the house like a fat dancer waiting for the call.
You are embarrassed, that you're not embarrassed.
150 cats live under the house with its
endlessly beautiful dripping sink.
Clouds line up
in shapes of food you no longer eat.
Your cats are all named Smith or Chevy.
Rice cakes, birds,
a phone in a chocolate cake.
Things are stunning.
If you had children they would gnaw
the ground like
sky that can't decide to eat us.
You sentimentally open a can of sardines,
and each sardine has its own television.
The cats have chewed the tires off your car.
Hope for anything remarkable and delicious
but the last orange you open is dry,
the cells empty as an abandoned jail.

Too bad those footprints on the moon
were made by moon boots.
Where are the barefoot girls?

Where are the Italian leather heels
and the cigarette butts?
Around here, suburban kids

walk to school in moon boots
like bits of charming plastic.
Where are the beat up leather shoes?

Where are the sandals made
of Colombian hemp? There are only
moon boots, golf balls, tire tracks.

All around its surface, the moon appears
the same up close as it does far away.
Long after we've had our impact,

moon boots, golf balls, tire tracks.
Go ahead. Look around. Take a step.
This is where I grew up. It appears

up close as it does far away.

WHITE BOWL

This morning, breakfast is lightning,
heavy air, hours-old eggs
dried up like a mud flat.

She has left me egg shells
drowned in the noise of a white bowl:
an elegance of the incomplete.

Like a collection of infant dreams
lifting sharp with messages for the storm,
I'll just step out and look for her.

I peer past doors leaning in frames
to the wallpaper of used-up smells,
rooms where the hard heat rooted in.

I feel like a small, unemployed miner.
More flashes at the window. A leg pokes out.
An arm dangles. There is nowhere to sit.

When the peal of thunder stops,
I pick up a hammer to raid the silence,
ready to break the first bird's song.

I'll take a shower. No, I'll take a shower outside in the leaves. I'll take a shower among the leaves with three naked women. In a thunderstorm. Yes, I'll take a shower with warm water and cold water and the leaves steaming around four naked bodies. I'll watch. I'll watch the three nymphs bathe in a raging ancient forest under a hot-springs waterfall. Then I'll join them with coconut milk. Wait, I'll take a shower in warm coconut milk with one woman and some lightning and a waterfall to watch in the distance. We could have our clothes on, wait for them to soak through with coconut milk, then rip them off in a crack of thunder. There will be drums and parrots. There will be drums and eagles. There will be a string quartet and screeching osprey. There will be nightingales and a small acoustic combo. There will be Robert Bly reading my poems, drunk on coconut milk, declaring me a genius, while a screeching raptor pecks out his entrails. I'll take a shower with milk and a nimble nymph under a waterfall at all times of the day and people will pay money to see it. The monks will join and throw rose petals. I'll take a shower with a coconut covered nymph and a choir of Krishnas to the music of the New Criterion Banjo Orchestra. The whole populous of Toronto will take a shower with the whole populous of Buffalo in Niagara Falls and I and the nymph will watch from a leaf covered cliff drinking coconut milk from a cistern in the shape of Robert Bly's head, while the screeching eagle will become the symbol for international peace and harmony. No, I'll take a bath.

ABOUT THE AUTHOR

PHOTO BY CHRISTINE HOLBERT

Scott Poole lives near Spokane, Washington with his wife and son. He is the associate director of Eastern Washington University Press. This is his first book.

ACKNOWLEDGMENTS

I want to thank Christopher Howell for his guidance, skill, enthusiasm and long, long hours of help with each one of these poems. I want to thank Nance Van Winckel for her never-ending encouragement. I am grateful to James McAuley for his guidance. I want to thank my parents, Bob and Cheryl Poole, for making me possible and supporting my dreams. Eternal thanks goes to mentors Dave Poole and Dr. Ricardo Sanchez who taught me the power of words in everyday life. Finally, my undying love and gratitude to my wife Leslie. You are the reason this book exists.

The author wishes to thank the editors of the following magazines in which some of these poems first appeared: *Fireweed, Dream International Quarterly, Poetic Express, Heliotrope, Spout, The Horsethief's Journal, George and Mertie's Place, The Temple, In Vivo, Musing, Blue Penny Quarterly, The Blue Moon Review, The Seattle Review,* and *The Mississippi Review.*